AF723805

Caring for **Grandma**

Tamara Lawrence

Caring for Grandma

© 2026 by Tamara Lawrence
All rights reserved.

No part of this book may be reproduced, distributed, or transmitted in any form or by any means, including photocopying, recording, or other electronic or mechanical methods, without the prior written permission of the author, except in the case of brief quotations embodied in reviews and other noncommercial uses permitted by copyright law.

Published by Loretta Lane Publishing

Text © 2026 by Tamara Lawrence
Illustrations © 2026 by Trevaughn L.

Illustrations by **Trevaughn L.**

Printed in the United States of America
First edition

ISBN (Hardcover): 979-8-9946029-0-4
ISBN (Ebook): 979-8-9946029-1-1

This book is dedicated to our dear grandma Loretta Evans, who taught us to keep our heads to the sky.

Table of Contents

1

My Grandma

The first time I ever realized what "life" was—that people are alive, and that I was alive—was with my grandma. I was ten years old. I lived with my mom, sister, and two brothers. Like most kids, I went to school and hung out with friends. I loved to dance, play basketball, and watch funny YouTube videos. And I loved my grandma. She moved in with us when she was eighty-two—really old when I think about it now but at the time, she never seemed old to me. She lived with us through the last few months of her life and I never expected to become a caregiver. I didn't even know what that meant! But becoming a caregiver made me appreciate life and it made me appreciate my grandma.

My grandma was smart, fashionable, and helpful to everyone she knew. She loved jazz music and attending live theater. Some of her favorite plays were *A Raisin in the Sun* and *The Color Purple*. She told me going to see plays would make me more cultured and said she wanted to take me. *Blah. Theater*, I thought.

"Why can't we just go to the movies?" I asked.

"Live theater can be so much more exciting," she said, her eyes lighting up like fireflies on a warm summer night. "You never know what to expect and you get to experience the story as if you're right there!"

I understood *exactly* what my grandma meant when she took me to see *The Lion King*. I wanted to be just like Nala and sitting in that theater I felt like I was a part of the jungle!

Sometimes my grandma took me to church where she was a deacon, helping with the finances and day-to-day activities. She would dress up in fancy hats, some with feathers and some with funny looking buckles, always with matching gloves. A few times she took me shopping to buy nice outfits for church too. Like a peacock showing off its big colorful feathers, the women at church presented their "best self before God," as my grandma would say. And she was always one of the best dressed.

My grandma enjoyed learning so much that she even went back to school in her 60s! Her favorite subjects were psychology, the way people feel and act, and **gerontology**, the study of old age and the problems with aging. I always remembered her reading the newspaper and filling out crossword puzzles to keep her mind thinking. Her friends called her the "queen of crossword puzzles."

In her free time, my grandma did a lot of volunteering. She volunteered with the Red Cross during neighborhood fires, where she would take her vest, flashlight, and emergency kit to assist people hurt in a house fire. She also worked with the hearing impaired and at marathons passing out water.

My grandma always made sure to check up on her older friends who were in the hospital or sick at home. These people are sometimes referred to as the "sick and shut in." She visited them in the hospital, bringing them gifts and praying with them. Every year she would send holiday cards to her friends who couldn't leave their homes. "I want all my friends to feel loved and remembered," she would say. I wonder if she knew she would become sick and shut in herself.

★★★

2

Grandma Gets Sick

My grandma lived alone and did many things on her own. She drove herself to the grocery store, to Bible study, and to hair and nail salons. If she did need help getting around, my sister would take her to the mall and doctor's appointments. Sometimes I would tag along too!

As my grandma grew older, traveling to her favorite places like the theater and church became difficult. Like many older people, her body started breaking down. She began having more aches and pains and had to walk with a cane. She remained in and out of the hospital because of weak bones, heart problems, and a crooked spine. I also noticed my grandma couldn't stand up straight anymore and started walking with a hunched back. She didn't complain much, so I just thought these were normal things that happened to older people. But I did wonder if my body would do the same one day.

When she was too hurt to leave home, my grandma donated money to her church and other organizations, like The National Association for the Advancement of Colored People, or NAACP, which is an *amazing* civil rights organization. She also had a meal delivery service bring her food to make eating easier. Once a week my mom, brothers, sister, and I brought over food and a movie to share. My favorite movie to bring over was *The Help.* With my grandma's movement more and more limited, it was important she still stay connected to the world. So even though she couldn't come out of her house I always made sure to go to hers.

My grandma didn't want my family, or me, to know how much pain she was in.

"How are you doing, grandma?" I would ask when I visited.

"My back hurts a little but I'm okay," she would say, her voice shaking while cracking a pained smile.

Eventually, she could no longer hide her pain. There were times she fell down at home and couldn't get up. One time my grandma took a bath and didn't have the strength to get out of the tub. She later told us it took her three hours to get out. Other times she fell, she had to crawl to the phone and call my mom and brothers to pick her up. It was scary to know she could be in danger and have no one to help. When my grandma stopped being able to walk without falling, my mom decided it was best for her to move in with us. This was the first time I heard the word "**caregiver"** and I had no idea what it meant. I would soon find out.

★ ★ ★

3

Grandma Moves In

By the time my grandma moved in she looked very unhealthy. She was almost as thin as a pole and fragile like a vase. Her fingers were twisted instead of straight and her voice creaked like a rusty gate. She never needed a wheelchair before she moved in, but now it was the only way she could get around.

I was happy I was going to see my grandma more often but didn't know how my life would change. Would I have to move out of my room? Would I have to take care of my grandma now? Luckily my mom talked to me about these changes.

My mom revealed to me that my grandma had been gravely sick for a while. Her liver had **cancer** and her heart was weak.

"What exactly does that mean? What does it mean that she's sick?" I asked as my eyes welled up with tears. Cancer and a weak heart didn't sound good at all. "When people get old important parts of their body stop working," my mom answered gently, while wiping the tears running down my cheeks.

She wanted to be open and honest and told me to ask any more questions I might have about my grandma's illness.

"What does it mean to have cancer?" I asked.

"Grandma's cancer is a disease that caused a lump in the upper right part of her stomach and that lump is not supposed to be there. Her heart and blood vessels are not working the way they should either. The doctors say there is no treatment to cure her and we don't know how much longer she'll live."

When I heard that my heart sank. Cancer sounded scary enough. But the thought of my grandma dying left me feeling helpless. A special person in my family was sick and there was nothing I could do to make them better. *Why is this happening to my family?* I thought. But my mom reminded me there was something I could do. My grandma needed our family to take care of her and I was willing to do anything to make her feel better.

Even though we were all sad, my mom, sister, brothers, and I had to learn how to take care of an elderly person and we needed to work together. We also had to give up some of our own free time. My family was busy with work and school, but we had to slow down our personal lives to care for my grandma. My grandma was going to need full-time care, so we came up with a plan to all take turns helping. I didn't like seeing my grandma like this—but it made me appreciate the fact that I was healthy. And I hoped that someday when I got old, I would have a family who would take care of me like we were taking care of my grandma.

★ ★ ★

4

Grandma's New Routine

It took some time for everyone to adjust to our new lifestyle. We were now **caregivers**—people who are responsible for the care of a sick or disabled person. My grandma also had to get used to depending on others when for so long she did everything on her own. My mom said taking care of my grandma would take a lot of patience and understanding.

We started with changing my grandma's adult diapers. Because my grandma couldn't walk anymore, she used diapers instead of walking to the bathroom. As a team we helped change her, wiping her down and spreading ointment to keep the area moist. It was sort of like taking care of a baby. Even though she was an adult we had to be just as gentle.

My grandma's hands had **arthritis**. That's when a person's joints become stiff and painful. With the stiffness in her fingers, she couldn't always hold a fork, so we fed her. She loved my sister's cooking. "Thank you for the delicious food," she would say after every meal. Even though she was sick, my grandma always had nice manners.

Every day when I came home from school, I read books to my grandma. Our favorite books were *I Love My Hair, I know Why the Caged Bird Sings,* and *The Skin I'm In.* Some older people have a hard time reading or understanding written information, but it's important that they still exercise their mind. I would sit with her, point out the words I was reading, and ask what she thought about the story.

I also asked her to tell me stories about growing up in New York.

"Back then I used to love going to the movies for five cents!" she would say. She also told me about living through the Civil Rights Movement and her job inspecting parachutes during World War II. Hearing Grandma's stories was a great way to get to know her better while keeping both of our brains active. I loved hearing about my family's history too!

Before my grandma got sick, she always groomed herself, so my sister and I made sure to lotion her skin and brush her long gray hair. We painted her nails and sprayed her with her favorite perfume. We would also give her compliments like, "your hair is so pretty" and "you have great skin." Even though she was sick, it was important to her to still look good.

In the middle of the night my grandma would sometimes pull apart her diaper, leaving a big mess all over the floor. In the morning she wouldn't remember what she had done. This was a sign that she had **dementia**. That's when an older person has a difficult time thinking, remembering, and talking, and often gets angry or confused. At first, I was a little frustrated with my grandma for not remembering things and having to keep repeating myself. But I came to understand dementia is a disease, not my grandma's fault, and *it* was causing her to act differently. It was important to respond calmly and get my family's help if communicating was too hard. Teamwork was important when it came to caring for my grandma.

★ ★ ★

5

Grandma's Rehabilitation

My grandma needed **rehabilitation**, also known as **physical therapy**. This is a type of exercise treatment that helps people move better and build strength. When a person stays in bed for a long time their muscles can get thin, weak, and stiff. They can also get **bed sores**, which are painful wounds on the skin from the pressure of their weight. It was important to move my grandma around often to keep the blood flowing to her skin and help her body stay as healthy as possible.

On days she didn't feel too sick we would gently encourage my grandma to get out of bed and put her in her wheelchair. Then we would take her outside to get fresh air and sunlight and to stretch her arms and legs.

But sometimes she got very upset when we moved her around. She would hit us and even use bad words. "Don't touch me!" or "Get away from me!" she would yell. She wasn't being mean on purpose. She was in **chronic pain**, which meant she was hurting for a long period of time—every day. When someone is in constant pain, they may get irritated and **depressed**, which means feeling very sad or unhappy for a long time because of their pain. Every now and then I got scared because my grandma's mood could change so fast. I knew she couldn't control it, but it was hard to get used to. If my grandma's mood was too much to handle I made sure to tell my mom so she could take over.

We had to be understanding of how my grandma felt and the pain she was in. This is called having **empathy**, which means trying to understand how someone else feels by imagining what they might be going through. Instead of getting upset my sister and I sang and danced to make her happy. One of our favorite songs was *Single Ladies* by Beyonce. That also cheered us up because we did not like seeing my grandma hurt so much. It's important to find ways to have fun even in a stressful situation. Music and dance were a good way for me to express myself and release stress while still showing love to my grandma.

★ ★ ★

6

Grandma Gets Hospice Care

After several months, my grandma was getting sicker. Her heart and liver were no longer working properly. Her eyes turned yellow like egg yolks, her skin as pale as a ghost, and her hair was getting thinner.

The hospital sent **hospice care** to help us. This is a special type of help for people who are nearing the end of their life. Nurses and social workers come to the home of the very sick person, helping them have peace and comfort in their final days of living. They also give families medical, emotional, and spiritual support.

The nurses who came to my house would give my grandma medicine and keep her clean. They checked her **vitals** like her heart and lungs; brushed her teeth, gave her sponge baths, and gently turned her on her side so she wouldn't get bed sores. The social workers talked with us about our emotions and feelings. Sometimes we felt sad but other times we felt stressed, or angry, or confused. It was nice to have a safe place to talk about how I felt. The social workers made sure my family had all the emotional support we needed in caring for my grandma.

The nurses and social workers were very kind to my family. They helped make my grandma comfortable and gave us some relief from the hard work of caregiving. Being a caretaker can feel overwhelming, so having hospice workers there helped us feel less alone.

Soon after the hospice care visits began, my grandma stopped speaking and could not eat anymore. First, she was talking **incoherently**. That's when someone's speech is unclear, unorganized, and their words don't make sense. Then she could not communicate at all. All she could do was nod and blink. Her brain would not let her open her mouth. It was hard talking to someone who couldn't reply and trying to guess what they were thinking. My family still wanted my grandma to feel loved, so we did small things like hugging her, holding her hand, or sitting quietly beside her. I couldn't help but feel sad for her though and I missed my grandma's stories and her laugh, too.

★ ★ ★

7

Grandma and God

I didn't understand why my grandma wasn't getting better even though we were taking care of her. She was once full of energy and loved to learn. She enjoyed traveling and getting to know different cultures. Now she couldn't even talk or think clearly. I didn't think she deserved to be in so much pain.

My mom explained, "God doesn't give people problems they can't handle. That doesn't mean life won't be hard sometimes, but we will always have the strength to get through it. Struggles can even make you wiser and stronger in the end."

My mom also told me that hard situations can bring people closer to their family and God. She said, "Pain can help people see life more clearly and appreciate what really matters. It's how you *choose* to look at your situation." During this time, the most important thing was family. So, as a family we prayed for my grandma. Prayer gave us comfort and helped us feel closer to one another. I had never felt closer to my family than I did during this time.

My grandma believed in a higher power and a higher purpose. She used to say, "When you look down you see mud and dirt. When you look in front of you, you see the chaos of the world. But when you look up, you see something greater than us. So, I keep my head to the sky." We honored her belief in God by praying and keeping our heads up to the sky like she taught us. If my grandma could have still walked, she would have been at church until her very last day on this Earth.

★ ★ ★

8

Grandma's Last Day

One day after coming home from school, I went to check on my grandma before starting my homework. She couldn't really talk anymore but I made sure to say hello. A few hours later my mom went to see how my grandma was doing, but she sensed something was wrong. My grandma's breathing slowed down, and her head gently fell to her side. Next to my mom, my grandma took her last breath and made her transition to a better place.

At first, I couldn't believe it. I had never seen someone die and I didn't expect my grandma to pass away so soon. Even though I knew my grandma's life would one day end, it still came as a shock. All I wanted was to be next to my mom at this time.

My mom called my brothers and sister home to say goodbye to my grandma. Everyone cried, hugged each other, and talked about how much we would miss her. Then the **crematorium** workers came and took her away. These are people who turn bodies into sand, using a special, harmless process called cremation. They then return the sand in a nice vase so the family can keep a piece of their loved one.

Now my grandma was really gone. I knew I wouldn't be able to see her again, hear her voice, or touch her skin. That made me very sad and even a little angry. It was like my whole world sunk to the bottom of the ocean.

My mom told me it was normal to feel this way. These feelings are called **grief**. Sometimes people get mad when they feel someone special was taken away from them. They can also feel confused, lonely, and depressed. Not everyone experiences the same grief, but everyone has to go through it and take as much time as they need to heal.

To help me feel better my mom said I should draw pictures and write down stories about my grandma. Even though I couldn't see her anymore I would always have positive memories of her.

★ ★ ★

9

Grandma's Memorial

To honor my grandma's life, we had a "home-going" service, which some families call **funerals**. We invited all my grandma's family and friends to say their final goodbyes and to share how much they loved her. I got to make a short speech about the time I spent with my grandma and to express my feelings of sadness and love. I let everyone know how much she meant to me and told stories about fun times we had together.

At the service we had a band of African drummers perform. This tradition is believed to help the spirit move on from Earth and find its way to heaven. It can also give some healing for grieving family and friends while celebrating the life of the loved one who passed away. Along with music, everyone brought food to share. Food always brings people together and makes them feel comforted. My grandma would have wanted us to have a good time rather than only being sad.

I'm glad we got to celebrate my grandma in this way. She was a great woman with a lot of interests. She was kind, giving, and showed me so much love. My family was grateful to take care of her. In her last days of living she was not alone and was surrounded by loved ones. If we are blessed to live long enough, we will get old like my grandma. This is why we have family to love and to take care of each other.

Taking care of my grandma showed me that life is a gift and dying is a part of life. It's difficult to understand why people die but we have to accept it. It will be painful at first but will eventually get easier to live with. For me it hurts less and less each day but as my mom said, everyone deals with grief differently. My grandma will always live in my heart and that can never be taken away.

★ ★ ★

Glossary

Arthritis – when a person's joints become stiff, swollen, and painful, making it harder to move.

Bed sore – a painful sore on the skin caused by staying in one position for too long.

Cancer – a serious disease where unhealthy cells grow and spread in the body, making a person very sick.

Caregiver – someone who helps take care of a person who is sick, elderly, or needs extra support.

Chronic pain – pain that lasts for a long time and may happen every day.

Cremation – a special, harmless process that turns a body into sand, which is then returned to the family in an urn or vase.

Dementia – a brain condition that causes an older person to have a difficult time thinking, remembering, and talking.

Depression – a deep feeling of sadness that can last for a long time and affect how a person thinks and feels.

Empathy – understanding and caring about how someone else feels, even if you are not in the same situation.

Funeral – a ceremony held to honor and remember a person after they die.

Gerontology – the study of aging and the health needs of older people.

Grief – the sadness, anger, or confusion a person feels after losing someone they love.

Hospice care – a special type of help that focuses on comfort and peace for people who are very sick and nearing the end of their life.

Rehabilitation or **physical therapy** – an exercise treatment used to help people get back movement, strength, and independence.

Social worker – a trained helper who supports individuals and families with emotional, social, and life challenges.

Vitals – important signs of how the body is working, such as heart rate, breathing, and blood pressure.

★ ★ ★

Discussion Questions

Understanding Caregiving

1. What does it mean to be a caregiver?
2. Who were the caregivers in this story, and how did they help Grandma?
3. Why do you think caregiving can be both rewarding and challenging?

Feelings & Emotions

4. What different emotions did the narrator feel while caring for Grandma?
5. Have you ever felt confused, scared, or sad when someone you love was sick?
6. Why is it okay to have many feelings at the same time?

Empathy & Compassion

7. Why was Grandma sometimes angry or upset?
8. How did the narrator and her family show empathy toward Grandma?
9. What are some ways you can show kindness to someone who is having a hard day?

Coping & Self-Care

10. What activities helped the narrator cope with stress and sadness?
11. What are some healthy ways you can take care of yourself when life feels overwhelming?
12. Who can you talk to when your feelings feel too big to handle alone?

Grief & Healing

13. What is grief, and why does everyone experience it differently?
14. What helped the narrator remember Grandma after she passed away?
15. What are some ways families can honor and remember loved ones who have died?

Reflection & Connection

16. What is one lesson this story teaches about family?
17. What is one thing you learned about aging or caregiving from this book?
18. If you could say something to Grandma (or to someone you love), what would it be?

★ ★ ★

About Grandma Loretta

Loretta Evans was born in 1932 in the City of New York. She grew up in Sugar Hill, a neighborhood in Harlem, New York that was a popular place for African Americans to live. Many Black families moved there during the Harlem Renaissance, which was a movement of music, art, and literature. They wanted to create and celebrate their own culture in a time when Black people were treated unfairly. Loretta loved participating in the arts at this time.

Her favorite pastime was hanging out at her godparent's restaurant located across the street from the famous Apollo Theater. There she met some of her music idols like Harry Belafonte, Sarah Vaughan, and Sammy Davis Jr. Sammy and Loretta were friends, and he once invited her to be the president of his fan club.

At the age of 12 Loretta worked inspecting parachutes during World War II, the biggest mass war in history. Her job was to check parachutes for holes to make sure they would work properly for soldiers jumping out of airplanes. She was saving the lives of the soldiers because as they jumped, they needed their equipment to work properly.

Loretta had a flair for fashion. Her hats, shoes, and gloves were always perfectly coordinated. In her early twenties she even modeled for different designers and strutted down many New York runways.

Loretta took her education seriously. She was a true logophile, or someone who loves words. But being an intelligent young woman, she was very observant of the issues of the world, like racism. Racial segregation was common in the country and it moved her to try to end the injustice. She was motivated to always help others, spread goodwill, and stand up for silenced voices. She would always say, "You have to have the courage of your conviction to stand up for what you believe."

One way she fought for human rights was by joining the civil rights movement. She worked with supporters of all races to fight against social injustice. She picketed, boycotted, wrote letters, and organized rallies for freedom and equality.

Loretta believed that through education, she would be able to fight against social injustices. She went to Pace College and graduated in the School of Business with honors. She then earned another degree from Holy Names College, graduating in human services and psychology.

Loretta married Earle Evans and gave birth to her only daughter, Elise Evans, during the Civil Rights era. They modeled together and shared a love of travel, adventure, and the arts. They visited both coasts, went camping and skiing, and attended symphonies, operas, jazz concerts, and many plays. After eight years of marriage, Loretta became a single mother. She faced this new chapter with strength and determination, and did not allow it to define her limits.

With her love for education, Loretta aimed to empower the youth in San Francisco, where she and her daughter lived. For 24 years she worked behind the scenes in the school district to ensure students had equal opportunities to succeed.

Loretta was a lifetime learner. She enrolled in the Over-Sixty Program at San Francisco State University, where she studied gerontology and psychology.

In her mid-seventies, Loretta developed many health challenges that caused her body to slowly decline. Her eldest grandson, Julian, moved in to help assist her last few years of life. During the last three months of her life Loretta lived with her daughter, Elise, and grandchildren, Tamara, Damari, and Amara, who cared for her with love, patience, and devotion.

Loretta Evans passed away on March 26, 2015. She was surrounded by family and unconditional love until her very last day.

★ ★ ★

About the Author

Tamara Lawrence is an actress, model, and content creator from Oakland, California. She is a graduate of Loyola Marymount University, where she earned a degree in Communications. At a young age, Tamara traveled to nine countries and co-authored two theatrical plays, experiences that shaped her love for storytelling, culture, and human connection.

After college, Tamara returned to the Bay Area to help care for her grandmother during the final years of her life. Becoming a caregiver deeply impacted her understanding of family, aging, and compassion, and ultimately inspired her to write *Caring for Grandma*.

Through this story, Tamara hopes to give young readers language for difficult experiences such as illness, caregiving, grief, and loss—while honoring the strength and dignity of elders.

Drawing on her background in performance and digital media, Tamara now uses content creation to foster healing, reflection, and connection within families. She continues to live and create in the Bay Area.

★ ★ ★

www.ingramcontent.com/pod-product-compliance
Ingram Content Group UK Ltd.
Pitfield, Milton Keynes, MK11 3LW, UK
UKHW061034310726
14089UKWH00010B/236
* 9 7 9 8 9 9 4 6 0 2 9 0 4 *